Introducing
Eastern
Wildflowers

Written and Photographed by E. BARRIE KAVASCH

ISBN 0-88839-092-0
Copyright © 1982 E. Barrie Kavasch

Canadian Cataloging in Publication Data
Kavasch, Barrie E.
Introducing eastern wildflowers

(Northeast color series)
ISBN 0-88839-091-2

1. Wildflowers - Northeastern States - Ident-
ification. 2. Wildflowers - Canada, Eastern
- Identification. I. Title. II. Series.
QK118.K38   582.13'0974
C81-091080-2

Editor Margaret Campbell
Production/Design Peter Burakoff
Layout Diana Lytwyn
Typeset by Anne Whatcott in Megaron type on an AM Varityper
Comp/Edit
Printed in Canada by Friesen Printers

Published by

Hancock House Publishers
256 Route 81, Killingworth, CT, U.S.A. 06417
Hancock House Publishers Ltd.
19313 Zero Avenue, Surrey, B.C., Canada V3S 5J9

Table of Contents

ACKNOWLEDGMENTS............. 4
WORDS OF CONSERVATION 5
INTRODUCTION 6
Bloodroot 7
Dutchman's Breeches 7
Squirrel Corn 8
Early Saxifrage 8
Clintonia / Corn Lily 9
Large-flowered Bellwort 9
Solomon's Plume 10
Painted Trillium 10
Wood Lily 11
Turk's Cap Lily 11
Round-Lobed Hepatica 12
Rue-Anemone..................... 12
Red Baneberry 13
Wild Columbine................... 13
Pink Lady's Slipper 14
Yellow Lady's Slipper.............. 14
Dwarf Ginseng 15
Toothwort / Pepperwort 15
Downy Yellow Violet............... 16
Common Blue Violet 16
Johnny-Jump-Ups 16
Wild Geranium 16
Herb Robert 17
Pinxter Flower 17
Jack-in-the-Pulpit 17
Common (Wild) Strawberry 18
Steeplebush...................... 18
Bee Balm / Oswego Tea 19
Wild Bergamot   19

Mountain Mint 19
Enchanter's Nightshade 20
Black Cohosh 20
Great Lobelia..................... 20
Lady's Thumb 21
Soapwort Gentian................. 21
Fringed Gentian 21
Swamp Candles 22
Butterfly Weed.................... 22
Pinesap 23
Soapwort / Bouncing Bet 23
Bladder Campion 24
Spiderwort 24
Rabbit-Foot Clover 25
Horse Nettle 25
Spotted Knapweed 26
Sneezeweed 26
Prairie Blazing Star 26
Jerusalem Artichoke 27
Bull Thistle 27
New York Ironweed 27
Whorled Wood Aster 28
Calico / Starved Aster 28
Small White Aster 28
Flat-topped Aster 28
New England Aster................ 29
Bushy Aster 29
Turtlehead 29
FURTHER READING 30
INDEX 31
AUTHOR'S PROFILE 32

Acknowledgments

My special appreciation to Sterling and Ruth Parker, Rejean Metzler, Bea Hessel, and the Roxbury-Bridgewater Garden Club for inspiring many aspects of my long love affair with the wildflowers. Some of these plants were photographed on various Audubon Sanctuaries, and in the Native Plant Arboretum on the grounds of the American Indian Archaeological Institute in Washington, Ct. The rest were photographed throughout the northeast, and in wildflower gardens, as well as on private and public sanctuaries. My personal regards to each of these places, and to the many special people and botanical societies who have assisted my work. Very sincere esteem to the herbariums in the east which have deepened my research interests, and to the special people who tend them.

Much love to my talented family, who share my love of wildflowers, and to David Hancock for urging this book into being.

With respect,
E. Barrie Kavasch
Bridgewater, Connecticut
October 1980

Large White Trillium

Words of Conservation

It is hard to believe that our wildflowers are a fragile breed of flora and need to be protected. Especially in April when you come upon a vast bank of Bloodroot and Dutchman's Breeches blossoming in great profusion. Or in May when woodland areas seem blanketed in Pink Lady's Slippers and Dwarf Ginseng. Hard, indeed, to realize that their incredible beauty endangers them.

People still come up to me after my wildflower lectures and say "... but where are the Pink and Yellow Lady's Slippers in early Spring? And, the Fringed Gentians in late Fall? I used to be able to find them blossoming in such great quantities that, as a child, I could pick wonderful bouquets and take them home to enjoy." Truly, if each of us helped ourselves, soon there would be none left for anyone to enjoy! In fact, it is easier and cleaner to collect those unbelievable wildflowers with the camera, or sketch pad and pencils. Each species is a delicate and comprehensive work of art. Be careful not to trample or alter their habitats; remember that most of them take many years to develop and spread in any appreciable numbers. Love and awareness are very important. Note and enjoy, but *DO NOT PICK OR DIG UP THE WILDFLOWERS* in their natural areas.

Wildflower gardens are a growing fashion, especially among conservationists and naturalists, but also at industrial plants, corporate facilities, schools and historical museums. Most of our wildflowers can be purchased (in seed or plant form) from well-known wildflower nurseries throughout the northeast. This is truly the renaissance for native flora.

Only through understanding, caring and conservation can we insure our native wildflowers for our future generations.

Turtlehead

Introduction

Spring in New England is the most intensive and extraordinary season for wildflowers. People come from all over the world to view our flora, as others come in October to appreciate our Autumnal colors. This richness and diversity of botanical beauty has been recreating these varied panoramas for countless centuries.

Summer and Fall bring various combinations of wildflower blossoms, followed by their various seed pods, berries, nuts and climax materials (what remains of the spent blossoms on their stalks. . . often woody and easily preserved). They weave a rich botanical tapestry, each plant fulfilling itself at its own pace, in its own distinct season, and each necessary to specific biomes and habitat areas within the cycle of life.

This small guide focuses on the broad range of native flora, but includes a few introduced species that have become very important and widespread in the east. It is interesting to view the various wildflowers in the context of their specific families, not as a scholarly exercise but as a way of realizing their relationships to each other, and to the general spectrum of eastern flora.

It is always exciting to take just one area of botany and work intensively with it. This is my recurring, annual pleasure with wildflowers. I enjoy photographing their changing growth forms, and following them seasonally. I delight in sketching and drawing them, and in some cases, pressing them at various stages to preserve them for use in the herbarium. Through this book I share this with you, and invite you to enjoy some of our exquisite wildflowers!

Dog Tooth Violet or Trout Lily

1 BLOODROOT
Sanguinaria canadensis

Poppy Family

This fragile, white, perennial wildflower of early Spring opens in the sun and closes each night (or cloudy day). Bloodroot favors moist, rich woodlands. This native herb is widely spread throughout the northeast. The plant is notorious for its acrid orange-red juice which was used to dye clothing and baskets (by the Amerindians), and above all as a body paint. It had the additional benefit of being an insect repellent. This small member of the Poppy Family colonizes whole areas where its soft foliage — large, multi-lobed, veined leaves — dominates throughout most of the growing season. Their erect, oval, green capsules ripen in early Summer and hurl their tiny pearly seeds some distance from the parent plants, thereby ensuring good spread of this species.

2 DUTCHMAN'S BREECHES
Dicentra cucullaria

PAPAVERACEAE
Poppy Family

Distinctive, fragrant, white flowers arranged along a slender arching stalk give this early Spring wildflower its classic name. The feathery-fine, grayish green, deeply-cut leaflets are spread beneath the rows of blossoms like a network. These delicate native plants are on the protected list in most areas, and *should never be dug up or picked up*, unless "salvage botany" dictates in an area to be used or changed by construction.

1

1 SQUIRREL CORN
Dicentra canadensis

PAPAVERACEAE
Poppy Family

Sister wildflower to the Dutchman's Breeches, the foliage and growth habits and habitats are so identical that only the flowers distinguish them for the interested observer. Also, the tiny roots resemble kernels of yellow corn in this species. This wildflower seems to be much less common today, placing it on the endangered species list in many states.

2 EARLY SAXIFRAGE
Saxifrage virginiensis

SAXIFRAGACEAE
Saxifrage Family

Fragrant, white clusters of tiny flowers reach above the branched, sticky, hairy stalks that rise from a basal rosette of hairy, oval leaves no more than a few inches off the ground. This early harbinger of Spring creates beauty in mossy, rocky areas. This petite botanical has numerous relatives which are cultivated in shaded rock gardens.

1

2

3 CLINTONIA
or CORN LILY
Clintonia borealis

Shiny, basal, green leaves offset the smooth stalk bearing yellowish-green, bell-like flowers. This lovely Spring wildflower favors moist, acid woods. This botanical is well known again in Autumn for its three to six vivid blue berries, which are considered poisonous. Also known as "Blue Bead Lily," its generic name honors an early New York governor, DeWitt Clinton (1769-1828).

4 LARGE - FLOWERED BELLWORT
Uvularia grandiflora

LILIACEAE
Lily Family

Tall, slender, drooping, yellow blossoms terminate their smooth arching stems. The bell-like flowers are enhanced by light green foliage. The stalkless leaves clasp and embrace the stalk in a most distinctive manner. Here in dry, acid woods it is flanked by newly-emerging Wild Sarsaparilla, *Aralia nudicaulis,* young leaf-stalk on one side and new flower stalk on the other.

3

4

1 SOLOMON'S PLUME

LILIACEAE
Lily Family

Similacina racemosa

   Long, shiny, green leaves alternate along a smooth arching stem, which bears a creamy-white, pyramidal cluster of tiny flowers at its tip. This graceful wildflower seeks the same woods and clearings as its relative the true Solomon's Seal, *Polygonatum biflorum*. They are easily recognized by their different flower presentations. The latter has paired, greenish-yellow, axillary blossoms which dangle, bell-like, from the leaf joints.

2 PAINTED TRILLIUM

LILIACEAE
Lily Family

Trillium undulatum

   This is one of our most attractive woodland wildflowers. The erect, stalked, white flowers have a brilliant splash of pink crowning their centers. These beauties seek swamps and moist, acid woods where they can spread in profusion. The trilliums should be protected and never dug or removed from their environments.

1

2

3 WOOD LILY
Lilium philadelphicum

LILIACEAE
Lily Family

Erect, smooth stems and whorled leaves support our showiest woodland lily. These brilliant orange flowers dominate their Summer meadows with robust beauty. This is a bulbous perennial favorite that earlier people used and ate, but it is protected and admired for its beauty today.

---

4 TURK'S CAP LILY
Lilium superbum

LILIACEAE
Lily Family

A tall, sturdy, flowering stem bears numerous, nodding, brilliant orange, spotted blossoms. Strongly recurved petals distinguish this species as our largest, showiest native lily. Blooming through late Summer,these perennials seek wet, acid environments.

3

4

Perhaps nothing makes a meadow more valuable or lovely than its flowers.

1   ROUND-LOBED HEPATICA

Hepatica americana

RANUNCULACEAE
Buttercup Family

These early Spring wildflowers are graceful additions to our dry, rocky woods. Radiant lavender-pink blossoms stand on hairy stalks only a few inches above the ground. Their low foliage is a mass of dark green, shiny leaves, which were believed to resemble the liver. Because of this they are sometimes called "Liverworts." They are unrelated to the true liverworts, however.

2   RUE-ANEMONE

Anemonella thalictroides

RANUNCULACEAE
Buttercup Family

A delicate woodland perennial with two or three white blossoms on slender stalks above a whorl of small, dark green, three-lobed leaves. This widespread wildflower is frequently cultivated in rock gardens.

1   2

Rue the cold and welcome Spring with its wealth of early wildflowers to carpet woods, meadows, trails and roadsides.

3 **RED BANEBERRY**
Actaea rubra

RANUNCULACEAE
Buttercup Family

Bushy, dark green foliage offsets the delicate blossom spire of tiny, creamy-white flowers. Tall yet lacy, this showy native wildflower favors woods and thickets. Its shiny red berries are highly poisonous, as are those of its sister herb, White Baneberry, *Actaea pachypoda*, sometimes called "Doll's Eyes."

4 **WILD COLUMBINE**
Aquilegia canadensis

RANUNCULACEAE
Buttercup Family

Nodding red and yellow flowers dangle on tall, slender stalks above light green, fine, three-lobed foliage. These elegant Spring wildflowers are popularly admired. Their drooping, bell-like blossoms with their deeply sculptured nectar tubes (or spurs) attract long-tongued insects. Columbines are a widespread native perennial, seeking woodland borders and thickets along rocky slopes. This species is very similar to our garden varieties, which are cultivated in colors ranging from lavender purple to pale pinks.

3

4

1 PINK LADY'S SLIPPER
Cypripedium acaule

ORCHIDACEAE
Orchid Family

A distinctive, pink, slipper-like, inflated lip petal, veined with cherry red, forms this unusual flower. It usually sits alone at the top of a stalk above long, ribbed, dark green leaves that are silvery underside. Also called "Mocassin-Flower," this is our largest native orchid, and is widely spread in the northeast. It blossoms in late Spring, in dry woods. Like our other native orchids *these should never be picked,* and *they do not transplant well* into wildflower gardens.

2 YELLOW LADY'S SLIPPER
Cypripedium calceolus

ORCHIDACEAE
Orchid Family

An inflated, shiny yellow, slipper-shaped lip petal is back-fastened to spirally-twisted, greenish-yellow side petals. These exotic blossoms, often fragrant, are borne atop slender stalks above their oval, parallel-veined leaves. Throughout late Spring these showy native orchids blossom in rich, damp woods and bogs where they can form considerable populations, just like the previous orchid. *These blossoms should never be picked.*

1

2

3 DWARF GINSENG
Panax trifolium

ARALIACEAE
Ginseng Family

Tiny umbels of white blossoms rise above a whorl of three compound leaves during late Spring. This diminutive perennial seeks moist woods, often colonizing small areas, and looks like a small version of Ginseng. The tiny blossoms ripen to clusters of yellowish berries.

4 TOOTHWORT
or PEPPERWORT
Dentaria diphylla

CRUCIFERAE
Mustard Family

These charming early Spring wildflowers project terminal clusters of white to pink blooms atop erect stems. Their deeply-cut leaves with three-toothed lobes are lovely foliage. These dainty botanicals often colonize in moist woods, and are noted for their peppery sap and the tooth-like projections on their underground stems (rhizomes).

3   4

Fragile carpets of wildflowers cover woodland floors, inviting spring pollinators, artists and photographers, and especially appreciators.

1 DOWNY YELLOW VIOLET
Viola pubescens
2 COMMON BLUE VIOLET
Viola papilionaceae
3 JOHNNY-JUMP-UPS
Viola tricolor

VIOLACEAE
Violet Family

These three species are among our showiest and most often seen Spring violets. There are almost 900 species found worldwide, and many are cultivated for their lovely blossoms within our gardens. Violets produce two distinctive types of flowers: the showy classic blooms with which we are familiar, and also a clistogamous, non-flowering, greenish-white bloomstalk and pod sometimes on or below the ground. Although these latter flowers do not bloom, they produce great quantities of seeds. These dainty herbs fill our woods, thickets and lawns with various colors throughout the Spring.

4 WILD GERANIUM
Geranium maculatum

GERANIACEAE
Geranium Family

Loose clusters of showy flowers in varying shades of pinks and lavenders ripen to leave behind distinctive seed pods reminiscent of a stork's bill, which is another popular name for these delicate perennial herbs. The deeply cut, lobed leaves are random shades of gray-green. This foliage is delicate but persistent, and remains to turn varying shades of brilliant reds in late Summer and early Fall.

1

2

3

4

5 HERB ROBERT
Geranium robertianum

GERANIACEAE
Geranium Family

Tiny, paired, pink to lavender flowers supported on sturdy, erect stalks are flanked by deeply-cut palmate foliage. This miniature member of the geranium family blooms all Summer long in hardy profusion. This herb is a widespread native which seems content in many different types of habitats.

6 PINXTER FLOWER
Rhododendron nudiflorum

ERIEACEAE
Heath Family

This native "pink azalea" is a fine deciduous shrub. Its terminal blossom clusters produce showy, faintly fragrant, tubular, trumpet-shaped flowers. Favoring dry, upland woods to swamps, this low, lovely shrub blossoms in late Spring. Its twigs, buds and leaves are relatively smooth and slender.

7 JACK-IN-THE-PULPIT
Arisaema triphyllum

ARACEAE
Arum Family

This is a classic woodland wildflower, whose true blooms are tiny male and female flowers hidden deep within the lovely striped spathe ("pulpit") at the base of its enclosed spadix ("Jack"). When properly fertilized by flies and various crawling insects they produce this distinctive cluster of shiny red berries on the spadix by late Summer. The long stemmed, three-parted, veined leaves are usually dull green. In one variety, Woodland Jack-In-The-Pulpit, *Arisaema atrorubens,* the typical leaves are gray-green underneath. In the Northern Jack-In-The-Pulpit, *Arisaema stewardsonii,* also known as "Indian Turnip," the Spring spathe tube is corrugated with white ridges, not the reddish-brown to purple type you see here. These were special food plants to the Amerindians.

5

7

6

7

17

1 COMMON (WILD) STRAWBERRY

Fragaria virginiana

ROSACEAE
Rose Family

Open fields and woodland borders invite this native herb, which will often spread in low patches by putting out runners. The small, white Spring blossoms stand on hairy stalks above their three-part toothed leaves. The small flower centers enlarge with fertilization to a fleshy cone, which gradually sinks beneath the foliage and ripens and reddens into the finest, sweetest wild strawberries. Our cultivated varieties of strawberries are hybrids which were developed from this native stock.

2 STEEPLEBUSH

Spirea tomentosa

ROSACEAE
Rose Family

Also called "Hardhack," this lovely, native, meadow perennial blooms from the top downward, in a showy, branched spire of tight, pink flowers. The leaves of this erect woody shrub are oblong, toothed, veined and deep green with a bronze woolly underside. Low areas and old meadows throughout the northeast support several species of these showy Summer wildflowers. Their finished bloom spires persist as clusters of tiny, woody capsules. As climax material these cuttings are lovely for dried flower arrangements.

1

1

**3 BEE BALM
or OSWEGO TEA**
Monarda didyma
4 WILD BERGAMOT
Monarda fistulosa

LAMIACEAE
Mint Family

Such distinctive, brilliant red, tubular flowers surround these rounded terminal heads, at the tops of the unique square stems. The reddish bracts beneath each flower cluster offset the long, ovate, coarsely-toothed leaves, which are highly fragrant. This tall, stately native wildflower is a perennial favorite in moist or dry rocky habitats. Spreading by its creeping roots, Bee Balm will sometimes colonize a whole area, or take off and spread through a meadow. More often you will find the pale lavender to pink *Monarda fistulosa,* which is an ubiquitous meadow resident. These lovely erect herbs are a slightly smaller version of Bee Balm, but just as wonderfully aromatic. Both species are excellent tea plants, and their dried leaves make delicious seasonings and condiments.

5 MOUNTAIN MINT
Pycnanthemum virginiana

LAMIACEAE
Mint Family

Branching, flat-topped clusters of dense, roundish, silver-white heads (on which a few florets bloom at a time) crown tall, slender, square stems. Fine, multi-branched foliage with grass-like leaves radiate in opposite arrangements off the stem. The whole plant is highly aromatic when gently rubbed. There are fifteen species of these native perennials in New England. They spread through meadows and thickets colonizing whole biomes where suitable. These native herbs are being brought in from the wild and cultivated by people who are finding them new and exciting to grow and use. The climax blossoms and stalks dry beautifully for Winter bouquets, and the foliage dries for teas and culinary uses.

3

5

4

5

1 ENCHANTER'S NIGHTSHADE

Circaea quadrisulcata

ONAGRACEAE
Evening Primrose

You are probably most familiar with this woodland wildflower in Fall when its tiny, bristle-covered, oval green seeds stick (like sticktights) to your clothing and your dog's hair. During Summer these small, spreading terminal clusters produce tiny, two-petalled, white flowers on slender green stalks, above smooth, thin, dark green leaves. The foliage is nicely toothed and leaves tend to decrease in size as they grow closer to the flower clusters. This common native wildflower favors damp, rich woods and is broadly spread throughout North America.

2 BLACK COHOSH

Cimicifuga racemosa

RANUNCULACEAE
Buttercup Family

Also known as Bugbane, this tall, lacy, perennial, woodland wildflower spreads through rich woods in the northeast. Long, narrow spires of white flowers attract numerous pollinators. The plant's foliage has a very unpleasant odor which seems to repel bugs (hence its second name). This is a large plant, blooming throughout Summer, and a well-spread native in the northeast.

3 GREAT LOBELIA

Lobelia siphilitica

CAMPANULACEAE
Bluebell Family

Rich, open woods and meadows are the habitats in which to seek these showy, bright blue wildflowers. The distinctive blossoms are in the leaf axils, and sometimes form clusters around their tall bloom spire, which can reach 100 centimeters (39 inches) high. This native species flowers through late Summer and Fall, and is widespread in the eastern areas. There are many lobelias, but the most vivid is our native, *Lobelia cardinalis,* which loves damp sites throughout the northeast. Its brilliant red, tubular blooms form elongated clusters along their slender stalk. Hummingbirds are its key pollinators.

1

2

4 LADY'S THUMB
Polygonum persicaria

POLYGONACEAE
Buckwheat Family

This abundant, naturalized weed is found throughout North America along roadsides and in meadows and damp clearings. The dense erect spikes of tiny purple to pink flowers top slender jointed stems. The smooth narrow leaves sometimes have a dark green triangle in their middle that is said to resemble a lady's thumb print. This is one of several that bloom throughout the Summer until killed by frost.

5 SOAPWORT GENTIAN
Gentiana saponaria

GENTIANACEAE
Gentian Family

Dark blue, cylindrical, bottle-like blossoms form a tight cluster at the terminal of their dark green stem. Smooth, shiny, lily-like leaves offset these distinctive wildflowers. This particular species is named for its soapy juice. Blossoming in late Summer and into Fall, these herbs seek moist, shaded habitats.

6 FRINGED GENTIAN
Gentiana crinita

GENTIANACEAE
Gentian Family

Striking, fringed, deep blue flowers crown this usually petite wildflower. These exquisite blossoms open during the day and close at night (mimicking the internal time-clock of many early Spring wildflowers). The tubular flowers are composed of four flaring petals emerging from a distinctly four-sided calyx. The deep green foliage is relatively insignificant, being perhaps intimidated by the blossoms. The small leaves are opposite and slender, lance-shaped with pointed tips. The Fringed Gentian is one of our last Eastern wildflowers to bloom in the Autumn. It favors wet meadows and stream banks. This species is becoming increasingly rare, and *must not be picked.*

4

5

6

1 SWAMP CANDLES
Lysimachia terrestris

PRIMULACEAE
Primrose Family

Tall, slender branched, terminal clusters of many yellow blooms with red encircling the centers distinguish this perennial wildflower. Swamp Candles favor wet areas and are well spread throughout the northeast. These bright herbs hybridize freely with other loosestrifes, and bloom through Summer.

2 BUTTERFLY WEED
Asclepias tuberosa

ASCLEPIADACEAE
Milkweed Family

Bright orange clusters of small flowers fill a central crown at the top of the leafy, hairy stem. The oblong, narrow leaves, when broken, exude a watery sap, unlike the milky latex known to most of the milkweeds. Blooming throughout the Summer in dry, open habitats, this herb is frequently grown from seeds in home wildflower gardens to attract butterflies. This lovely herb, whose roots were chewed by the Amerindians to treat pleurisy, is also known as "Pleurisy Root." It is closely related to the Purple Milkweed, *Asclepias purpurascens,* which seeks moist, rich environments, and is also a great attraction to the butterflies and other pollinating insects.

1

2

Summer wildflowers grow strong and vivid. Their bright blossoms mass to enhance the most ragged growing areas.

PINESAP
Monotropa hypopitys

MONOTROPACEAE
Indian Pipe Family

These unusual herbs are considered saprophytic, in that they do not photosynthesize for energy, but obtain nourishment from certain fungi associated with the roots of trees. Amber, slightly translucent, almost succulent, nodding flowers top a scaly, leafless stem. As the flowers ripen their heads gradually rise to face straight up. Pinesap emerge during Summer in acid woods, and usually beneath oaks or pines. These are closely related to the Indian Pipes, *Monotropa uniflora,* which is a waxy white plant found singly to very densely clustered. The Indian Pipes have just a single nodding flower, as their species name implies. Like the Pinesap, these herbs ripen their seeds when their heads stand erect. In age this plant gradually turns brownish black, as the fruits ripen. This form becomes almost woody and will persist throughout Winter.

SOAPWORT
or BOUNCING BET
Saponaria officinalis

CARYOPHYLLACEAE
Pink Family

Dense white to pinkish, throated flowers with five petals form terminal clusters on smooth, sturdy, leafy stems. The blossoms are most fragrant in the evening, when they attract night-flying pollinators. This beautiful, introduced, widespread perennial herb spreads rapidly using creeping underground stems, and can form considerable colonies at roadsides and in meadows. Blooming throughout Summer into Fall, the entire plant can be crushed and rubbed to create a soapy, green lather, which is excellent for washing fabrics and dishes.

4

1 BLADDER CAMPION
Silene cucubalus

CARYOPHYLLACEAE
Pink Family

The balloon-like, veined calyx behind the fragrant, white blossoms distinguishes this Summer perennial. It is a favorite meadow and roadside wildflower, widely distributed throughout the east, along with eight other related species. These herbs are also principally fragrant in the evening.

2 SPIDERWORT
Tradescantia virginiana

COMMELINACEAE
Spiderwort Family

Bright violet, tri-petalled flowers with distinct yellow stamens nest together in a terminal cluster. These are flanked by long, narrow, folded, iris-like leaves. This showy spiderwort derives its name from its terminal bud cluster which resembles a squatting spider. The vivid blossoms are usually open only in the early half of the day. The versatile spiderwort is widely acclaimed today as "the flower of the anti-nuclear movement" because geneticists have found it can detect radiation and relay details of pollution through definite blossom color differences. These plants can also detect pesticides, auto exhausts and sulphur dioxides. Native perennials of roadsides and meadows, the spiderwort has been cultivated for its unique beauty for centuries. Now it is receiving great attention, and it is being cultivated all over America, especially around nuclear installations. The ethnobotany of the 1980s is wisely using plants as indicators.

1

Evening walks are specially fragranced by the evening-blooming wildflowers such as Soapwort and Evening Primrose.

3 RABBIT-FOOT CLOVER
Trifolium arvense

FAGACEAE
Pea Family

    Soft, fuzzy, pink-tinged to gray cylindrical flowerheads top silky stems above their narrow, elliptical leaflets. Both blossoms and foliage of this delicate but hardy annual herb decorate roadsides and the borders of old fields with their short showy masses. This is one of my favorite clovers, in a family of many beauties. These plants dry well to make lovely Winter bouquets.

4 HORSE NETTLE
Solanum carolinense

SOLANACEAE
Nightshade Family

    This coarse, native, thorny perennial has white, star-like flowers with distinct yellow centers. The rough leaves are long, multi-lobed, and covered with prickles. Not a favorite weed, this insidious nightshade does have aspects of beauty. The starry blooms set small, yellow, tomato-like berries, and though attractive, they are toxic and should not be picked or eaten.

3   4

1 SPOTTED KNAPWEED
Centaurea maculosa

ASTERACEAE
Sunflower Family

A multi-branched, wiry-stemmed herb with radiating, lavender-pink, thistle-like flowers. This brilliant, low, spreading wildflower has naturalized to fields and roadsides, where it provides a profusion of color in Summer. Spotted Knapweed, along with several other species of Knapweeds, are widely spread throughout the northeast, from Canada to South Carolina, and moving out to the midwestern states.

2 SNEEZEWEED
Helenium autumnale

ASTERACEAE
Sunflower Family

The brilliant, yellow, daisy-like flowers have scalloped, fan-shaped rays that droop backward like elegant petticoats, accentuating the disk flowers in a conspicuous green ball at the center. The dark green leaves alternate along the winged stalk. As the species name implies, this intriguing wildflower blossoms in Autumn, favoring swamps, pond borders and wet areas. The common name refers to the use of the dried leaves for snuff during colonial times, when inhaling the powdered herb would cause sneezing . . . beneficial to purge the body of evil spirits.

3 PRAIRIE BLAZING STAR
Liatris pycnostachya

ASTERACEAE
Sunflower Family

Densely crowded, rose-magenta disk flowers crowd closely along a thick, erect, very tall stalk. Numerous long, slender leaves intersperse this tight, showy arrangement. Though not native to the northeast, this is one of our most popular Blazing Stars, and it is often cultivated in wildflower gardens for its striking color, posture and height (to 150 centimeters — 60 inches). It blooms from Summer through Fall, and loves damp environments.

1

Quite a family!   2

4 JERUSALEM ARTICHOKE

Helianthus tuberosus

ASTERACEAE
Sunflower Family

Very tall (to 300 centimeters — 120 inches) thick, hairy stalks with large, thick, rough, alternate leaves offset terminal branches which bear large yellow flowers. These perennial native sunflowers prosper in most environments, and have spread throughout our range. Cultivated by the Amerindians for their nutritious edible tubers (which contain no starch), these sunflowers are widely sought for their dramatic height, edibility and beauty.

5 BULL THISTLE

Cirsium vulgare

ASTERACEAE
Sunflower Family

This is our spiniest and tallest (to 180 centimeters — 72 inches) biennial thistle, and produces large, showy, magenta disk flowers, which attract numerous interesting pollinators. These Great Spangled Frittilaries are but a few of its many visitors. Bull Thistles blossom throughout the Summer and prefer old pastures and roadsides all over the northeast. The bristly foliage is also very attractive, and this dramatic wildflower is often cultivated for these features, as well as to attract the birds, bees and butterflies.

6 NEW YORK IRONWEED

Veronica noveboracensis

ASTERACEAE
Sunflower Family

Deep violet-lavender flower clusters form branched sprays of blooms at the summit of these tall (to 180 centimeters — 72 inches) meadow herbs. The plant is a bit rough, but graceful with alternate, slender, pointed leaves. Blossoming almost until frost, this rugged native perennial favors moist environments and is well spread through southern New England.

1 WHORLED WOOD ASTER
Aster acuminatus
2 CALICO
or STARVED ASTER
Aster lateriflorus
3 SMALL WHITE ASTER
Aster vimineus
4 FLAT - TOPPED ASTER
Aster umbellatus

These four of our most prominent white asters populate various environments in the northeast, from dry, barren soils to swamps, and from hot, sunny meadows to rich, deciduous woods. They represent one of our largest native perennial wildflower families, and are widespread. They bloom from August through October, and hybridize so easily with each other that sometimes it is difficult for botanists to tell one species from another. The first is one of our most petite, and favors open woods. The next two prosper in meadows and thickets. The last is one of our tallest (to 210 centimeters — 84 inches), and favors wet areas.

1

2

5 **NEW ENGLAND ASTER**
Aster novae-angliae
6 **BUSHY ASTER**
Aster dumosus

ASTERACEAE
Sunflower Family

These two striking wildflowers represent the many different species of pale lavender to deep purple composite flowers that make up the other half of the Aster Family. Both of these favor moist regions. Their flower colors are quite variable, but they are constant bloomers: August through October, through most of our range. There are sixty-eight species with numerous varieties of these classic native perennials. Also known as "Starworts" and "Frost Flowers" the asters have long histories of usage among Amerindians and colonists.

---

7 **TURTLEHEAD**
Chelone glabra

SCROPHULARIACEAE
Figwort Family

A terminal cluster of white, lavender-tinged, tubular flowers (which resemble turtleheads) crown this smooth long-leaved plant. Throughout late Summer this intriguing wildflower blossoms in wet habitats. It is widely distributed in the northeast.

5

6

7

Further Reading

FERNALD, Merritt L. *Gray's Manual of Botany. Eighth Edition.* NYC: D. Van Nostrand Co. 1970.

KAVASCH, Barrie. *Botanical Tapestry.* Washington, Ct.: Gunn Historical Museum. 1979

NIERING, William A. and Olmstead, Nancy C. *Audubon Society Field Guide to North American Wildflowers.* NYC: A.A. Knopf. 1979.

PETERSON, Roger T. *Field Guide to the Wildflowers.* Boston: Houghton Mifflin Co. 1968.

Spotted Knapweed

Index

taea rubra 13	Herb Robert 17
emonella thalictroides 12	Horse Nettle 25
uilegia canadensis 13	Jack-in-the-pulpit 17
saema triphyllum 17	Jerusalem Artichoke 27
clepias tuberosa 22	Johnny-jump-ups 16
ter acuminatus 28	Lady's Thumb 21
ter dumosus 29	Large-flowered Bellwort 9
ter lateriflorus 28	Liatris pycnostachya 26
ter novae-angliae 29	Lilium philadelphicum 11
ter umbellatus 28	Lilium superbum 11
ter vimineus 28	Lobelia siphilitica 20
e Balm 19	Lysimachia terrestris 22
ack Cohosh 20	Monarda didyma 19
adder Campion 24	Monarda fistulosa 19
oodroot 7	Monotropa hypopitys 23
uncing Bet.......................... 23	Mountain Mint 19
ll Thistle 27	New England Aster.................... 29
ushy Aster 29	New York Ironweed 27
tterfly Weed......................... 22	Oswego Tea 19
lico Aster 28	Painted Trillium 10
ntaurea maculosa 26	Panax trifolium 15
elone glabra 29	Pink Lady's Slipper 14
micifuga racemosa 20	Pepperwort 15
caea quadrisulcata 20	Pinesap 23
rsium vulgare 27	Pinxter Flower 17
ntonia 9	Polygonum persicaria 21
ntonia borealis 9	Prairie Blazing Star 26
ommon Blue Violet 16	Pycnanthemum virginiana 19
ommon Wild Strawberry 18	Rabbit-foot Clover 25
orn Lily 9	Red Baneberry 13
pripedium acaule 14	Rhododendron nudiflorum 17
pripedium calceolus 14	Round-lobed Hepatica................. 12
ntaria diphylla 15	Rue-anemone 12
centra canadensis 8	Sanguinaria canadensis 7
centra cucullaria 7	Saponaria officinalis 23
wny Yellow Violet.................... 16	Saxifrage virginiensis 8
utchman's Breeches 7	Silene cucubalus 24
varf Ginseng 15	Similacina racemosa 10
rly Saxifrage 8	Small White Aster 28
chanter's Nightshade 20	Sneezeweed 26
at-topped Aster 28	Soapwort 23
agaria virginiana 18	Soapwort Gentian.................... 21
inged Gentian 21	Solanum carolinense 25
ntiana saponaria 21	Solomon's Plume 10
ntiana crinita 21	Spiderwort 24
ranium maculatum 16	Spirea tomentosa 18
ranium robertianum 17	Spotted Knapweed 26
reat Lobelia......................... 20	Squirrel Corn 8
elenium autumnale 26	Starved Aster........................ 28
lianthus tuberosus 27	Steeplebush......................... 18
patica americana 12	Swamp Candles 22

Toothwort.............................. 15
Tradescantia virginiana 24
Trifolium arvense 25
Trillium undulatum 11
Turk's Cap Lily 11
Turtlehead 29
Uvularia grandiflora 9
Veronica noveboracensis 27

Viola papilionaceae ....
Viola pubescens ....
Viola tricolor...........................
Whorled Wood Aster ....
Wild Bergamot.........................
Wild Columbine........................
Wild Geranium ....
Wood Lily..............................
Yellow Lady's Slipper...................

Author's Profile

   E. Barrie Kavasch is a self-taught naturalist and ethno-botanist with special interests in the plant world. She is an artist and photographer, and is also the author/illustrator of *Native Harvests* and *Botanical Tapestry,* as well as a *Guide to Eastern Mushrooms* and *Guide to Wild Edibles.* She lectures throughout New England, and demonstrates the harvesting and preparation of "wild edibles."
   Her love of the durable wild spreads into harvesting roots, seeds, vines, fungi and seaweed...in order to explore their special creativity in cordage and fiber-making, mat and basket weaving, making paints, inks, natural dyes, cosmetics and simple medicines.